# I HAVE GIVEN
# THEM THE GLORY

*Dear Dave,*
*We hope this blesses*
*you! In Christ,*
*Shannon and Jeff*
*Watson*

# I HAVE GIVEN THEM THE

# GLORY

## THOUGHTS ON CHRISTIAN UNITY

JIM WILSON

*edited by Lisa Just*

COMMUNITY
CHRISTIAN
MINISTRIES

Published by Community Christian Ministries
P.O. Box 9754, Moscow, Idaho 83843
208.883.0997 | www.ccmbooks.org

Jim Wilson, *I Have Given Them the Glory: Thoughts on Christian Unity*

Cover design by James Engerbretson.
Interior design by Valerie Anne Bost.
Printed in the United States of America.

18 19 20 21 22 23 24 2        9 8 7 6 5 4 3 2 1

*To Graham & Libby Gutsche,*
*close friends for sixty years*

# CONTENTS

Preface . . . . . . . . . . . . . . . . . . . . . . . . . . . . . . . . . . . . . . . . . . . . ix

Introduction . . . . . . . . . . . . . . . . . . . . . . . . . . . . . . . . . . . . 1

Chapter 1: The Pleasantness of Unity . . . . . . . . . . . . . . . . 5

Chapter 2: One in Christ . . . . . . . . . . . . . . . . . . . . . . . . . . . 7

Chapter 3: The Body of Christ . . . . . . . . . . . . . . . . . . . . . 17

Chapter 4: The Characteristics of Unity . . . . . . . . . . . . . 25

Chapter 5: Purity & Fellowship . . . . . . . . . . . . . . . . . . . . 27

Chapter 6: Hindrances to Unity . . . . . . . . . . . . . . . . . . . 37

Chapter 7: Love . . . . . . . . . . . . . . . . . . . . . . . . . . . . . . . . . 47

Chapter 8: Humility . . . . . . . . . . . . . . . . . . . . . . . . . . . . . 49

Chapter 9: Knowledge . . . . . . . . . . . . . . . . . . . . . . . . . . . 55

Chapter 10: One Mind............................61

Chapter 11: Disunity & Church Leaders ............ 63

Chapter 12: False Unity........................... 67

Chapter 13: Tradition............................ 77

Chapter 14: Reader Comments..................... 83

Conclusion...................................... 87

Appendix A: Assurances of Salvation .............. 89

Appendix B: The True Church..................... 99

# PREFACE

The primary assumption in this book is the authority and inspiration of the Scriptures. The promises, prayers, commands, and narratives are not up for consideration. They are to be believed and obeyed.

The Church is made up of individual members, separate parts of the body of Christ. This book is written to the parts, not to the whole. The Church cannot obey God as a single entity. Only the parts can obey.

I will quote many Scriptures without doing much exposition of the text. I hope to draw attention to the commands themselves so that we can realize that we are obeying them or not obeying them. If we realize that we are not obeying, I hope that we will also come to individually repent of our disobedience. If this seems hard to you, I suggest you read *How to Be*

*Free from Bitterness* and *How to Maintain Joy,* available at
www.ccmbooks.org or by calling Community Christian Ministries at (208) 883-0997.

In John 17, Jesus says, "My prayer is not for them alone. I pray also for those who will believe in me through their message, that all of them may be one, Father, just as you are in me and I am in you. May they also be in us so that the world may believe that you have sent me. *I have given them the glory that you gave me, that they may be one as we are one*: I in them and you in me. May they be brought to complete unity to let the world know that you sent me and have loved them even as you have loved me" (John 17:20-23).

Jesus gave us the glory so that we might be one. In the same paragraph, He tells the Father three times what kind of unity this is:

- Just as You *are* in Me and I am in You
- That they may be one as We *are* one
- I in them and You in Me

Twice He says why he is praying this: "so that the world may believe that You have sent Me."

God's glory in us is the basic provision for unity. This unity will let the world know that He came from the Father. Unity is the basis of world evangelism.

The church of Jesus Christ started in glory, unity, and prayer: "They all joined together constantly in prayer, along with the women and Mary the mother of Jesus, and with his brothers" (Acts 1:14). The result of this unity was preaching the gospel in the fullness of the Holy Spirit. The result of that was 3,000 new believers, soon followed by 2,000 more.

"After they prayed, the place where they were meeting was shaken. And they were all filled with the Holy Spirit and spoke the word of God boldly. All the believers were one in heart and mind. No one claimed that any of his possessions was his own, but they shared everything they had. With great power the apostles continued to testify to the resurrection of the Lord Jesus, and much grace was upon them all" (Acts 4:31-33). These Christians were filled with the Holy Spirit. They preached the Word boldly and were of one heart and mind.

In the last two centuries, there have been recurrences of this kind of oneness in prayer and preaching in power leading to conversions of thousands. In Wales in 1859, there were 110,000 new believers in a few months; this happened again in 1905 with another 70,000 believers. Similar events occurred in Korea, northern China, and India.

All over the world today, there are small groups who have oneness in prayer and Bible study. There are also hundreds of mission groups and thousands of missionaries whose emphasis is oneness in prayer and preaching the gospel.

The first instance of diversity in the Church occurred in Acts 6: "In those days when the number of disciples was increasing, the Grecian Jews among them complained against the Hebraic Jews because their widows were being overlooked in the daily distribution of food" (Acts 6:1).

The church took immediate action: "Brothers, choose seven men from among you who are known to be full of the Spirit and wisdom. We will turn this responsibility over to them and will give our attention to prayer and the ministry of the word" (Acts 6:3-4). This action was not political; it was spiritual. The men were selected not because they were popular, but because they were godly.

There was potential for disunity again in Acts 11 and Acts 15. It was stopped before it got started. Paul and Barnabas had a sharp disagreement in Acts 15:36-40, but it does not seem to have carried over to the churches.

The churches at Rome and Ephesus had serious problems keeping unity. We can see this from Paul's letters to them. In every case, corrective action was taken to maintain the unity of the body.

The New Testament Christians also tended towards disunity by becoming followers of teachers and people who possessed particular gifts. These issues are addressed in 1 Corinthians 1-3 and 11-14.

The Reformation was wonderful because of the multitude of people who were saved, but it was awful in the divisions. Since that time, there have been increasing numbers of divisions among those who believe in salvation by grace through faith in the person and work of the Son of God.

In the last three centuries, there have been hints of unity in different parts of the world. This unity has been manifested in four different ways: praying for each other, preaching the gospel together, singing together, and doing humanitarian work.

The Wesleyan revival in England, Scotland, and Wales in the mid-18th century and the Great Awakening in the same period were times of increased unity. The revivals in Wales especially brought great unity among Baptists, Congregationalists, Anglicans, Reformed Methodists, and Wesleyan Methodists. The Second Great Awakening in the 19th century led to the salvation of many but also resulted in many splinter groups. Today evangelistic works like the Scripture Union, CSSM, InterVarsity, Young Life, Youth for Christ, and the Officers' Christian Fellowship all dwell on the gospel of Jesus Christ to the benefit of the body of Christ.

## CHAPTER 1

# THE PLEASANTNESS OF UNITY

How good and pleasant it is when brothers
live together in unity! (Psalm 133:1).

Amen! That is clearly true. If you do not understand
it, think of the opposite: How bad and unpleasant it is
when brothers live together in disunity! The world's
solution to the problem of disunity is to quit living together. That is one of the primary reasons we have so
many denominations, but it is not a valid reason.

What is unity like? "It is like precious oil poured on
the head, running down on the beard, running down
on Aaron's beard, down upon the collar of his robes"

(Psalm 133:2). Unity is like being anointed with the Holy Spirit and the fruit of the Spirit. You might think that having oil poured on your head so that it runs down your face and your clothes would be very unpleasant. That is not the image! The image is of the first high priest being *anointed* with oil, perfumed and precious. *Messiah* (Hebrew) and *Christ* (Greek) both mean "the anointed one." The high priest was a figure of the true anointed one, Jesus. The priest was anointed with holy oil; Jesus was anointed with the Holy Spirit.

"It is as if the dew of Hermon were falling on Mount Zion. For there the LORD bestows his blessing, even life forevermore" (Psalm 133:3). Mount Hermon is over 9,000 feet high and is capped with snow. Unity is like the rain of that mountain falling on Jerusalem. For there (Zion, Jerusalem) the Lord will rain down His blessing. What is this blessing? Everlasting life, filled with the Spirit, which is the goodness and pleasantness of unity.

---

CHAPTER 2

# ONE IN CHRIST

Be completely humble and gentle; be patient,
bearing with one another in love. Make every
effort to keep the unity of the Spirit through
the bond of peace. There is one body and one
Spirit, just as you were called to one hope
when you were called; one Lord, one faith,
one baptism; one God and Father of all, who is
over all and through all and in all. (Eph. 4:2-6)

In any place, in any nation, the body of believers has always been made up of all saved people and no one who is unsaved. In Acts 1:15, the believers were "a group numbering about a hundred and twenty." Then Peter addressed the crowd at Pentecost. "Those who accepted his message were baptized, and about three thousand were added to their number that day" (Acts 2:41). We can draw several conclusions about this group of people: they were believers, and they were baptized. "And the Lord added to their number daily those who were being saved" (Acts 2:47).

After Peter's preaching in Acts 3, the number of believers increased again: "But many who heard the message believed; so the number of men who believed grew to about five thousand" (Acts 4:4). And again:

> Nevertheless, more and more men and women believed in the Lord and were added to their number. (Acts 5:14)

> In those days when the number of disciples was increasing. . . . So the word of God spread. The number of disciples in Jerusalem increased rapidly, and a large number of priests became obedient to the faith. (Acts 6:1, 7)

This increase was all in the church in Jerusalem. Notice that the Lord did the adding to the numbers. The people that were added were all saved. We do not know how many believers there were, except that their number exceeded 5,000. That number included men, women, and a large number of Jewish priests.

> They all joined together constantly in prayer, along with the women and Mary the mother of Jesus, and with his brothers. (Acts 1:14)

> Nevertheless, more and more men and women believed in the Lord and were added to their number. (Acts 5:14)

So the word of God spread. The number of disciples in Jerusalem increased rapidly, and a large number of priests became obedient to the faith. (Acts 6:7)

At first, the believers were mostly Jews, many of them expatriates, but the Church soon included many races, cultures, and nations:

While Peter was still speaking these words, the Holy Spirit came on all who heard the message. The circumcised believers who had come with Peter were astonished that the gift of the Holy Spirit had been poured out even on the Gentiles. (Acts 10:44-45)

The church sent them on their way, and as they traveled through Phoenicia and Samaria, they told how the Gentiles had been converted. This news made all the brothers very glad. (Acts 15:3)

After much discussion, Peter got up and addressed them: "Brothers, you know that some time ago God made a choice among you that the Gentiles might hear from my lips the message of the gospel and believe. God, who knows the heart, showed that he accepted them by giving the Holy Spirit to them, just as he did to us. He made no distinction between us and them, for he purified their hearts by faith. Now then, why do you try to test God by putting on the necks of the disciples a yoke

that neither we nor our fathers have been able
to bear? No! We believe it is through the grace
of our Lord Jesus that we are saved, just as
they are." (Acts 15:7-11)

At this point, the church was made up of thousands
of saved people with no apparent church membership
list. There were no deacons until later when a problem
ma-de them necessary. That problem was solved by
men filled with the Holy Spirit. Although the believers
met in various homes for breaking bread (Acts 2:46),
they were called the church (singular) in Acts 8:1-2.

The account of these things is in narrative form, so
it is not wise to derive doctrine from them. Church doctrine should come from the teaching and proclaiming
portions of Scripture. Here are two doctrinal decisions
made by the councils in Jerusalem:

"So if God gave them the same gift as he gave
us, who believed in the Lord Jesus Christ,
who was I to think that I could oppose God?"
When they heard this they were silenced.
And they glorified God, saying, "Then to the
Gentiles also God has granted repentance
unto life." (Acts 11:17-18)

It is my judgment, therefore, that we should
not make it difficult for the Gentiles who are
turning to God. (Acts 15:19)

The first council recognized that God had saved the
Gentiles who were in Cornelius' home and therefore
there could be no objection to Gentiles being in the

Church. The second council confirmed the decision of the first and ruled that the Gentiles who were turning to God did not have to be circumcised or keep the law of Moses. Circumcision was an entry rite and therefore *denied* as part of the gospel. Salvation is by the work of Jesus Christ received by faith alone. After they were saved, the Gentile Christians *were* required to abstain from food polluted by idols, abstain from sexual immorality, and abstain from blood and from the meat of strangled animals. The apostle Paul confirmed these decisions in his letters.

The narrative continues with stories of saved people being added to the Church.

> When they arrived, they prayed for them that they might receive the Holy Spirit, because the Holy Spirit had not yet come upon any of them; they had simply been baptized into the name of the Lord Jesus. Then Peter and John placed their hands on them, and they received the Holy Spirit. (Acts 8:15-17)

> Then the church throughout Judea, Galilee and Samaria enjoyed a time of peace. It was strengthened; and encouraged by the Holy Spirit, it grew in numbers, living in the fear of the Lord. (Acts 9:31)

> All those who lived in Lydda and Sharon saw him and turned to the Lord. (Acts 9:35)

> This became known all over Joppa, and many people believed in the Lord. (Acts 9:42)

The Lord's hand was with them, and a great number of people believed and turned to the Lord. (Acts 11:21)

He was a good man, full of the Holy Spirit and faith, and a great number of people were brought to the Lord. Then Barnabas went to Tarsus to look for Saul, and when he found him, he brought him to Antioch. So for a whole year Barnabas and Saul met with the church and taught great numbers of people. The disciples were called Christians first at Antioch. (Acts 11:24-26)

When the congregation was dismissed, many of the Jews and devout converts to Judaism followed Paul and Barnabas, who talked with them and urged them to continue in the grace of God. (Acts 13:43)

When the Gentiles heard this, they were glad and honored the word of the Lord; and all who were appointed for eternal life believed. The word of the Lord spread through the whole region. (Acts 13:48-49)

At Iconium Paul and Barnabas went as usual into the Jewish synagogue. There they spoke so effectively that a great number of Jews and Gentiles believed. (Acts 14:1)

But after the disciples had gathered around him, he got up and went back into the city. The next day he and Barnabas left for Derbe.

then to the Twelve. After that, he appeared
to more than five hundred of the brothers at
the same time, most of whom are still living,
though some have fallen asleep. (1 Cor. 15:1-6)

The gospel is:

- Jesus Christ is Lord.
- Christ died for our sins according to the Scriptures.
- He was buried.
- He was raised on the third day according to the
  Scriptures.

  It is because of him that you are in Christ
  Jesus, who has become for us wisdom from
  God—that is, our righteousness, holiness and
  redemption. (1 Cor. 1:30)

  For God so loved the world that he gave his
  one and only Son, that whoever believes in him
  shall not perish but have eternal life. (John 3:16)

  That if you confess with your mouth, "Jesus
  is Lord," and believe in your heart that God
  raised him from the dead, you will be saved.
  (Rom. 10:9)

What are the results of the gospel? Wisdom from God,
righteousness, holiness, redemption, forgiveness of sins,
salvation, everlasting life, and being born of the Spirit.

Truth: Everyone who is in the body of Christ has
received and believes in Jesus Christ. Truth: Everyone
who is in the body of Christ has received the fruit of
the Spirit. These two truths provide unity in the body.

Unity is broken when members of the body add to the gospel and call their additions sound doctrine. Sound doctrine is *the gospel only*. Unity is compromised when people who attend church and appear to be members of the body have not received Christ and therefore do not have the fruit of the Spirit. Since they do not know the Head, they are not real members of the body, but they try to interact as if they were.

Unity is also broken when members of the body do not walk in the light as He is in the light. "But if we walk in the light, as he is in the light, we have fellowship with one another, and the blood of Jesus, his Son, purifies us from all sin" (1 John 1:7). Unity is deep and close fellowship. This can only happen when everyone is walking in that same wonderful light.

Notice that our fellowship is with other believers and with the Father and the Son. This fellowship is not merely fun, food, and good conversation. It is deeper; it is fullness of joy. It is based upon receiving the person and work of Jesus Christ. "Yet to all who received him, to those who believed in his name, he gave the right to become children of God—children born not of natural descent, nor of human decision or a husband's will, but born of God" (John 1:12-13).

## CHAPTER 3

# THE BODY OF CHRIST

> Then we will no longer be infants, tossed back and forth by the waves, and blown here and there by every wind of teaching and by the cunning and craftiness of men in their deceitful scheming. Instead, speaking the truth in love, we will in all things grow up into him who is the Head, that is, Christ. From him the whole body, joined and held together by every supporting ligament, grows and builds itself up in love, as each part does its work. (Eph. 4:14-16)

This passage emphasizes two words: "love" and "grow." Two important phrases are "the whole body" and "each part." The whole body of Christ *grows* and *builds itself up in love* as *each part* (that is, each believer) does its work. This is how the body functions after it has been prepared by its pastors for works of service.

The only way pastors build up the body is by training saints to build each other up. (Of course, the pastors themselves are also members of the body and so are part of this building up.) Truth and love are the ingredients of this growth. Evangelists, pastors, and teachers are responsible for giving very much truth with very much love to the members of the body, which the members in turn give to each other.

Love without truth is like a body without bones. Truth without love is a body of nothing but bones. Pretend love and falsehood can also be mixed with truth. These three problems are visible in the church today.

Here is a clear sequence towards unity: 1) It was He who gave some to be apostles, prophets, evangelists, pastors, and teachers 2) to prepare God's people for the work of the ministry 3) so that the body of Christ may be built up until we all reach unity in the knowledge of the Son of God and become mature, attaining to the whole measure of the fullness of Christ. The direct cause of unity is *God's people* doing the work of the ministry. Building up the body of Christ is not the pastor's job. His job is to prepare God's people to do *their* job.

"To the church of God in Corinth, to those sanctified in Christ Jesus and called to be holy, together with all those everywhere who call on the name of our Lord Jesus Christ—their Lord and ours . . . " (1 Cor. 1:2). The Church is made up of all Christians everywhere. They should be meeting in local assemblies. However, the local assemblies may quarrel within themselves and with each other.

Local assemblies that deny, add to, or ignore the gospel of Jesus Christ are apostate or unbelieving churches. They are not dismembered parts of the body; they are not members of the body of Christ *at all*, and should not be considered Christians. We are not to be one with people who do not belong to Christ. Of course, there may be real Christians in the apostate churches. They are not functioning with other believers, but they should be.

The various parts of the body are all commanded to be immediately obedient to the Head, the Lord Jesus Christ. In many cases, believers obey their pastor or the rules of their "church," assuming that it is the same as being obedient to Christ.

Imagine that one hand represents one denomination, and the other hand represents another denomination, and the head tells the hands to clap. If the hands swing and miss each other, one or both hands have paid more attention to the arms or the wrists than to the head. They are disobedient. If our own bodies functioned like the body of Christ does today, we would all be in the hospital.

If someone is not acting like a Christian, is it possible to tell if he is not a part of the body or if he is just a part that is not functioning properly? There is no absolute way, because both situations look alike. Unbelievers can pretend to be believers; these are hypocrites. Christians can *act* like unbelievers; these are compromisers.

In a loving, gracious way, we should tell the compromisers *and* the hypocrites that we do not think they are saved. They may be offended and tell us not to judge.

> The acts of the sinful nature are obvious: sexual immorality, impurity and debauchery; idolatry and witchcraft; hatred, discord, jealousy, fits of rage, selfish ambition, dissensions, factions and envy; drunkenness, orgies, and the like. I warn you, as I did before, that those who live like this will not inherit the kingdom of God. (Gal. 5:19-21)

> But the fruit of the Spirit is love, joy, peace, patience, kindness, goodness, faithfulness, gentleness and self-control. Against such things there is no law. Those who belong to Christ Jesus have crucified the sinful nature with its passions and desires. (Gal. 5:22-24)

When we are saved, God transfers us from the first list to the second list. Ask them which list describes them best. If they say, "The first list," tell them that you agree with them and that Jesus Christ does a better job of saving than that. If they say they are in both lists, tell them that when they get out of the first list you will believe that they are Christians.

> Thus, by their fruit you will recognize them. (Matt. 7:20)

> What business is it of mine to judge those outside the church? Are you not to judge those inside? (1 Cor. 5:12)

If they are not part of the body, we want to help them find out. If they are part of the body, we want them to look like they are.

"The body is a unit, though it is made up of many parts; and though all its parts are many, they form one body. So it is with Christ. For we were all baptized by one Spirit into one body—whether Jews or Greeks, slave or free—and we were all given the one Spirit to drink" (1 Cor. 12:12-13). If we are born again, we are members of the body of Christ. It is *impossible* to be a member of the body of Christ *without* being a member of the local body, although you may not spend time with them. If we are immoral and unrepentant, we can be cut out of fellowship (1 Cor. 5), but we start out in fellowship at our new birth.

Today churches have two extremes of membership, neither of which are found in the New Testament:

Unsaved people are allowed to be members. We have let people "climb in by some other way" (John 10:1).

There are requirements for church membership in addition to salvation. These can include form of dress; length of hair; hair covering; a distinct eschatology; the "correct" systematic theology (e.g. Wesleyan, Reformed, Dispensational); form of worship; form and meaning of baptism; form of church government; following a certain leader; other "sacraments" and "ordinances."

It is more difficult to become a member of a local church than it is to become a member of the kingdom of God. In the New Testament, conversion alone automatically made people members of the local churches.

Churches full of saved people existed before there was such a thing as church government (Acts 14:23). Removal from the local church (other than by moving away) was based on unrepentant immorality (1 Cor. 5) or apostasy (1 Tim. 1:20). In both cases, the offender was "handed over to Satan to be taught not to blaspheme" (1 Tim. 1:20) so that "his spirit may be saved on the day of the Lord" (1 Cor. 5).

There is no biblical basis for church-membership requirements other than regeneration. Many churches have membership requirements in addition to professing faith in Christ. They want their members to believe in sanctification, the baptism of the Holy Spirit, eternal security, believers' baptism, infant baptism, predestination, pre-tribulation rapture, free will, etc. The awful part is that they think having these requirements is a good thing.

The new Christian does not know about any of these things, so he is enrolled in a new members' class where he is taught what is "right." He has no basis on which to disagree with what he is taught, so he agrees and becomes qualified to be a member. In the same new members' class, there may be an unsaved man who also agrees and is made a "member" based on that agreement. Such requirements exclude some who are truly Christians and include some who are not. They divide the brothers.

Why do churches have these requirements?

- They want their members to believe in the same kind of church government. The new members have to be taught it.

- They want their new members to have the same view of ordinances and sacraments. They must be taught these as well.
- They want their new members to have the same views of liturgy and church music. For this, they have to be taught *and trained*.
- They want their members to be of the same ethnicity, race, culture, or wealth.
- They want more members in order to get them to tithe to their church.
- They think they have to have "official" membership in order to exercise church discipline.

Many churches teach loyalty to themselves, not just to Christ. They insist upon loyalty so much that any "disloyalty" can lead to either church discipline or heavy false guilt laid upon the offender. This practice is strongly taught against in 1 Corinthians 1-3. Such partisanship is a sign of being worldly and "mere infants in Christ" (1 Cor. 3:1).

Remember what is of first importance: "For what I received I passed on to you as of *first importance*: that Christ died for our sins according to the Scriptures, that he was buried, that he was raised on the third day according to the Scriptures" (1 Cor. 15:3-4).

## CHAPTER 4

# THE CHARACTERISTICS OF UNITY

*Joy:* Rejoice in the Lord always. I will say it again: Rejoice! (Phil. 4:4)

*Purity:* But the wisdom that comes from heaven is first of all pure; then peace-loving, considerate, submissive, full of mercy and good fruit, impartial and sincere. (James 3:17)

*Kindness:* Be kind and compassionate to one another, forgiving each other, just as in Christ God forgave you. (Eph. 4:32)

*Gentleness:* A gentle answer turns away wrath, but a harsh word stirs up anger. (Prov. 15:1)

*Humility:* Be completely humble and gentle; be patient, bearing with one another in love. (Eph. 4:2)

*Peace:* Let the peace of Christ rule in your hearts, since as members of one body you were called to peace. And be thankful. (Col. 3:15)

*Patience:* Therefore, as God's chosen people, holy and dearly loved, clothe yourselves with compassion, kindness, humility, gentleness and patience. (Col. 3:12)

*Forgiveness:* Bear with each other and forgive whatever grievances you may have against one another. Forgive as the Lord forgave you. (Col. 3:13)

*Fellowship:* But if we walk in the light, as he is in the light, we have fellowship with one another, and the blood of Jesus, his Son, purifies us from all sin. (1 John 1:7)

*Righteousness:* The fruit of righteousness will be peace; the effect of righteousness will be quietness and confidence forever. (Isa. 32:17)

## CHAPTER 5

# PURITY & FELLOWSHIP

## Justification: The Basis for Fellowship

When we believed in Christ, we were made righteous. That is, we were justified: "Therefore, since we have been justified through faith, we have peace with God through our Lord Jesus Christ" (Rom. 5:1).

When we were justified, we became part of the one body of Christ, the Church:

> For we were all baptized by one Spirit into one body—whether Jews or Greeks, slave or free—and we were all given the one Spirit to drink. (1 Cor. 12:13)

> It is because of him that you are in Christ
> Jesus, who has become for us wisdom from
> God—that is, our righteousness, holiness and
> redemption. (1 Cor. 1:30)

All our sins were forgiven: "All the prophets testify about him that everyone who believes in him receives forgiveness of sins through his name" (Acts 10:43).

We received a new nature: " . . . and have put on the new self, which is being renewed in knowledge in the image of its Creator" (Col. 3:10).

We received eternal life: "For God so loved the world that he gave his one and only Son that whoever believes in him shall not perish but have eternal life" (John 3:16).

We were born of the Spirit: "Jesus answered, 'I tell you the truth, no one can enter the kingdom of God unless he is born of water and the Spirit'" (John 3:5).

We received the fruit of the Spirit: "But the fruit of the Spirit is love, joy, peace, patience, kindness, goodness, faithfulness, gentleness and self-control. Against such things there is no law" (Gal. 5:22-23).

At the moment of our salvation, we entered into fellowship with all other justified people. All at once, we had *purity, unity, and fellowship*. This happened to us after we received the proclamation of the good news: "We proclaim to you what we have seen and heard, so that you also may have fellowship with us. And our fellowship is with the Father and with his Son, Jesus Christ. We write this to make our joy complete" (1 John 1:3-4).

The Bible gives various descriptions of people before they receive Christ. These people may be church members, but there is no means of unity with them or within them. Here are a few examples of people who are on the outside of unity:

> The acts of the sinful nature are obvious: sexual immorality, impurity and debauchery; idolatry and witchcraft; hatred, discord, jealousy, fits of rage, selfish ambition, dissensions, factions and envy; drunkenness, orgies, and the like. I warn you, as I did before, that those who live like this will not inherit the kingdom of God. (Gal. 5:19-21)

> Furthermore, since they did not think it worthwhile to retain the knowledge of God, he gave them over to a depraved mind, to do what ought not to be done. They have become filled with every kind of wickedness, evil, greed and depravity. They are full of envy, murder, strife, deceit and malice. They are gossips, slanderers, God-haters, insolent, arrogant and boastful; they invent ways of doing evil; they disobey their parents; they are senseless, faithless, heartless, ruthless. (Rom. 1:28-31)

> Do you not know that the wicked will not inherit the kingdom of God? Do not be deceived: Neither the sexually immoral nor idolaters nor adulterers nor male prostitutes nor homosexual offenders nor thieves nor the greedy nor drunkards nor slanderers nor swindlers will inherit the kingdom of God. And that is what some of you were. But you

were washed, you were sanctified, you were justified in the name of the Lord Jesus Christ and by the Spirit of our God. (1 Cor. 6:9-11)

In reply Jesus declared, "I tell you the truth, no one can see the kingdom of God unless he is born again. . . . Whoever believes in him is not condemned, but whoever does not believe stands condemned already because he has not believed in the name of God's one and only Son. . . . Whoever believes in the Son has eternal life, but whoever rejects the Son will not see life, for God's wrath remains on him." (John 3:3, 18, 36)

For I tell you that unless your righteousness surpasses that of the Pharisees and the teachers of the law, you will certainly not enter the kingdom of heaven. (Matt. 5:20)

## Walking in the Light

Purity is a must for having fellowship and unity with other believers. Sin destroys fellowship. The Bible has two expressions of purity. They are *righteousness* and *holiness*. Holiness is purity that does not get dirty. Righteousness is impurity that has been cleansed. God gives us righteousness when we are forgiven. Then He requires that we continue to walk in purity, that is, that we be holy.

The way to stay pure is to walk in the light. "This is the message we have heard from him and declare to you: God is light; in him there is no darkness at all. . . .

But if we walk in the light, as he is in the light, we have fellowship with one another and the blood of Jesus, his Son, purifies us from all sin. . . . If we confess our sins, he is faithful and just and will forgive us our sins and purify us from all unrighteousness" (1 John 1:5, 7, 9).

God is light! We are to live in the light as God is in the light. We are to be *that* close to Him. If you and I live in that light, two things happen: 1) We have fellowship with each other. If you are in the light and I am in the light, it is impossible to not have fellowship. 2) God purifies us from all unrighteousness.

How do we walk in the light? The key is in verse 9: "If we confess our sins . . . " The way to have perfect fellowship with each other is to have all our sin and all our unrighteousness purified. We receive this purification by confessing our sins.

The only thing that can break our fellowship with God and with each other is sin. When we received Christ, all our sins were forgiven. At that point, we had a clean slate. But if we accumulate unconfessed, unforgiven sins, fellowship is ruined and unity greatly hindered. We are still part of the body of Christ, but the body is sick. If we do not confess our sins and receive God's cleansing, we may not hold anyone else responsible for our lack of unity.

If we walk in the light, we cannot help having fellowship. Roy Hession, a well-known evangelist, talks about walking in the light this way:

> To walk in the light is the opposite of walk-
> ing in darkness. Spurgeon defines it in one of

his sermons as "the willingness to know and be known." As far as God is concerned, this means that we are willing to know the whole truth about ourselves, we are open to conviction. . . . Everything He shows us to be sin, we will deal with as sin—we will hide or excuse nothing. . . . In 1 John 1:7, of course, the purpose of "walking in the light" is that we might "have fellowship with one another." And what fellowship it is when we walk this way together! Obviously, love will flow from one to another when each is prepared to be known as the repentant sinner he is at the cross of Jesus.[1]

The blood of Jesus cleansed us from sin when we were saved, and it keeps on cleansing us. Forgiveness of sin is not a one-time event. If we want to walk with God, we must be willing to be honest with Him about our sins and come to Him with them every day. If we are not being continually cleansed, we will be a disunited, dysfunctional body. Unity *requires* confession of sin.[2]

Unity and fellowship are not based on everyone agreeing with each other. They are based on our initial purification, justification, and entrance into the body of Christ and our walking in the light and being continually cleansed.

There is a better way to be clean than being cleansed. It is not getting dirty in the first place. That is called *holiness*.

1   Hession, Roy. *The Calvary Road*. Fort Washington, PA: CLC Publications, 1990, pp. 38-42.
2  For more on this, please read *How to Maintain Joy* at www.ccmbooks.org.

My dear children, I write this to you so that you will not sin. (1 John 2:1)

As obedient children, do not conform to the evil desires you had when you lived in ignorance. But just as he who called you is holy, so be holy in all you do. (1 Pet. 1:14-15)

Therefore, I urge you, brothers, in view of God's mercy, to offer your bodies as living sacrifices, holy and pleasing to God—this is your spiritual act of worship. Do not conform any longer to the pattern of this world, but be transformed by the renewing of your mind. Then you will be able to test and approve what God's will is—his good, pleasing and perfect will. (Rom. 12:1-2)

But I tell you: Love your enemies and pray for those who persecute you, that you may be sons of your Father in heaven. He causes his sun to rise on the evil and the good, and sends rain on the righteous and the unrighteous. If you love those who love you, what reward will you get? Are not even the tax collectors doing that? And if you greet only your brothers, what are you doing more than others? Do not even pagans do that? Be perfect, therefore, as your heavenly Father is perfect. (Matt. 5:44-48)

Do you want to be holy? When I ask Christians this, I get all kinds of evasive answers:

"It is impossible, so the question is irrelevant."

"If it means being like so-and-so, no."

"I think legalism is wrong."

"I don't want to be out of step with the evangelical culture. If I were holy, I would lose my Christian friends."

"My beliefs suit me just fine."

"I want to be right in my theology more than I want to be holy."

Do you want to be holy? If you cannot give a clear "Yes," you are saying that you do not want unity, at least not at the expense of your doctrine or your pride.


## Purity in the Church

> I have written you in my letter not to associate with sexually immoral people—not at all meaning the people of this world who are immoral, or the greedy and swindlers, or idolaters. In that case you would have to leave this world. But now I am writing you that you must not associate with anyone who calls himself a brother but is sexually immoral or greedy, an idolater or a slanderer, a drunkard or a swindler. With such a man do not even eat. What business is it of mine to judge those outside the church? Are you not to judge those inside? God will judge those outside. Expel the wicked man from among you. (1 Cor. 5:9-13)

Expel the wicked man from among you. At first glance, this might look like breaking unity, but it is not. The unity (i.e., the fellowship) was broken when the sin occurred. This man needs to be removed for two reasons: 1) If he is not removed, the acceptance of his immorality will infect the whole church. 2) If he is removed, he may repent and be saved. Breaking fellowship with unrepentant, immoral people in this way preserves the spiritual purity of the church, the real cause of unity.

## CHAPTER 6

# HINDRANCES TO UNITY

## Not Loving the Brothers

God gave us two basic commands related to the body of Christ: get into the body and function as a body. "And this is his command: to *believe* in the name of his Son, Jesus Christ, and to *love one another* as he commanded us" (1 John 3:23). 1) Believe in the name of His Son. 2) Love one another.

The basic problem of the body of Christ is that it is not following the second command. This is very serious. If we do not love each other, we have every reason to doubt that we are in the body.

> We *know* that we have passed from death to life, because we love our brothers. Anyone who does not love remains in death. (1 John 3:14)

We love because he first loved us. If anyone says, "I love God," yet hates his brother, he is a liar. For *anyone who does not love his brother,* whom he has seen, *cannot love God,* whom he has not seen. And he has given us this command: Whoever loves God must also love his brother. (1 John 4:19-21)

A new command I give you: Love one another. As I have loved you, so you must love one another. *By this all men will know that you are my disciples, if you love one another.* (John 13:34-35)

If we love, we build up the body. If we do not love, we are either not part of the body or we are acting like we are not part of it.


## Unconfessed Sin

Sin of any kind is the primary cause of disunity and broken fellowship. *Unconfessed* sin causes continual disunity. Sins like stealing, murder, rape, and lying are easy to recognize, but if they are not confessed, the result is disunity. Sins like borrowing and not returning, lust, harboring hatred in your heart, and exaggerating the truth are harder to recognize and thus less likely to be confessed. Result: disunity. Abstract sins like envy, jealousy, and bitterness are even harder to recognize and even less likely to be confessed. Result: disunity.

## Teachers

Teachers can be a major hindrance to unity. This applies even to teachers of the truth who have no differences with each other, as in 1 Corinthians 1 and 3. Their followers were spiritual infants because they were loyal to a single teacher. It also applies to teachers who are seeking their own following, as Paul predicted would happen in Ephesus: "I know that after I leave, savage wolves will come in among you and will not spare the flock. Even from your own number men will arise and distort the truth in order to draw away disciples after them" (Acts 20:29-30).

Scripture records several other occurrences of teachers provoking disunity:

> They said to you, "In the last times there will be scoffers who will follow their own ungodly desires." These are the men who divide you, who follow mere natural instincts and do not have the Spirit. (Jude 18-19)

> Then we will no longer be infants, tossed back and forth by the waves, and blown here and there by every wind of teaching and by the cunning and craftiness of men in their deceitful scheming. (Eph. 4:14)

> But avoid foolish controversies and genealogies and arguments and quarrels about the law, because these are unprofitable and useless. Warn a divisive person once, and then warn him a second time. After that, have nothing to do with him. You may be sure that

such a man is warped and sinful; he is self-condemned. (Titus 3:9-11)

I urge you, brothers, to watch out for those who cause divisions and put obstacles in your way that are contrary to the teaching you have learned. Keep away from them. For such people are not serving our Lord Christ, but their own appetites. By smooth talk and flattery they deceive the minds of naive people. (Rom. 16:17-18)

These teachers are still around today. They are a problem, but so are the people who follow them: "A horrible and shocking thing has happened in the land: The prophets prophesy lies, the priests rule by their own authority, *and my people love it this way*. But what will you do in the end?" (Jer. 5:30-31). Christians love to follow new teaching without searching the Bible first to see whether it is true or false. They love to be unique. They are not eager to maintain unity.

### Church Government

There was great disunity in the church in England and Scotland during the first half of the 17th century. The church was divided into three main groups: the Church of Scotland, the Church of England, and the dissenters (nonconformist congregational churches). All three churches were evangelical, and all three were reformed. Why were they divided? State and church government! The Church of Scotland was a state church with a Presbyterian government. The Church of England was a state church with an Episcopalian government. The Congregationalists wanted to have nothing to do with the state. The Church of Scotland was only willing to unite with the Church of England if they had a Presbyterian government. The Church of England was willing to unite with the Church of Scotland only if Scotland would adopt the Episcopalian form of government. And of course they wanted the dissenters to be in that church, too. So they went to war. England won and forced its bishops on the Scots.

The Puritans who came to Massachusetts during this time were dissenters from England who did not want to be in the state churches of England or Scotland, but once they were in Massachusetts, they immediately set up a state church of their own.

Three of the thirteen colonies allowed freedom of religion, even though they were founded by people with a definite religion. They were Rhode Island (founded by Roger Williams, a Baptist), Pennsylvania (founded by William Penn, a Quaker), and Maryland (founded by Cecil Calvert, Lord Baltimore, a Roman Catholic).

The disunity in England and Scotland was not an issue of doctrine, but of who was in control. It was driven by the pride of man and by being loyal to men rather than to God.

## Confessions

The creeds put together by the early Church were written either to separate Christians from non-Christians (e.g., the Apostles' Creed) or to separate Christianity from Christian heresies (e.g., the Nicene Creed and the Athanasian Creed).

Later on, some of the Church councils included heresies in their own pronouncements. The Second Council of Nicea brought the veneration of images into the churches. The Council of Trent denounced those who believed in justification by faith alone as heretics. The First Vatican Council set as dogma the idea that the pope is infallible when he speaks *ex cathedra* and the notion of the immaculate conception of the Virgin Mary.[3]

After the Reformation, the whole Church no longer got together to form creeds. The different groups met separately and wrote confessions differing from or reacting to the other groups. Now confessions separate Christians from Christians.

This is a quote from the autobiography of Richard Baxter, who lived in the mid-17th century.

> I am more deeply afflicted for the disagreements of Christians than I was when I was a younger Christian. Except the case of the infidel world, nothing is so sad and grievous to my thoughts as the case of the divided churches; and, therefore, I am more deeply sensible of the sinfulness of those prelates and pastors of the churches who are the principal cause of these divisions. Oh, how many millions of souls are kept by them in

3  I.e., the notion that Mary was born sinless.

ignorance and ungodliness, and deluded by
faction as if it were true religion! How is the
conversion of infidels hindered by them, and
Christ and religions heinously dishonored!...
I am more sensible that most controversies
have more need of right stating than of de-
bating; and, if my skill be increased in anything, it is in that in narrowing controversies
by explication, and separating the real from
the verbal, and proving to many contenders
that they differ less than they think they do.[4]

## Divisions and Subdivisions

Denominations divide and subdivide on tradition, theology, ecclesiology, eschatology, worship, sacraments/
ordinances, evangelism, holiness, and loyalty. Local
churches also split over things like liking or disliking
the pastor, which family rules the church, the color of
the nursery walls, bitterness, the choir and/or praise
team, whether the pastor should wear an earring, jealousy, envy, and personal opinions.

Everyone who is divided on the first list would have
to change his mind and his actions in nearly every area
of his life in order to have complete unity in the body.
The difficulty is that everyone thinks they are right on
everything, so it is everyone *else* who needs change.

Here is another difficulty. Suppose all Christians
everywhere agreed on everything and no one differed

4  *The Autobiography of Richard Baxter.* Ed. N.H. Keeble. Rowman &
Littlefield, 1974; pp. 157-8, 161.

with anyone else at all. No one would like it! Why? No one would get to be the *most right*.

In 1 Corinthians 1 and 3, Paul hit church divisions hard. The church had all the gifts of the Spirit (1 Cor. 1:7), but that did not make them spiritual. Paul said they were still worldly—infants in Christ. "Brothers, I could not address you as spiritual but as worldly—mere infants in Christ. I gave you milk, not solid food, for you were not yet ready for it. Indeed, you are still not ready. You are still worldly. For since there is jealousy and quarreling among you, are you not worldly? Are you not acting like mere men? For when one says, 'I follow Paul,' and another, 'I follow Apollos,' are you not mere men?" (1 Cor. 3:1-4).

Paul spoke again on the subject of divisions in chapter eleven: "In the following directives I have no praise for you, for your meetings do more harm than good. In the first place, I hear that when you come together as a church, there are divisions among you, and to some extent I believe it. No doubt there have to be differences among you to show which of you have God's approval" (1 Cor. 11:17-19). Is this approval? No! Paul's sarcasm is a strong denunciation of their differences. All of them are wrong. All of them need to repent.

### Divisiveness

This may sound like a contradiction, but God requires us to break fellowship with those who break fellowship.

> I urge you, brothers, to watch out for those
> who cause divisions and put obstacles in

your way that are contrary to the teaching
you have learned. Keep away from them.
(Rom. 16:17)

Warn a divisive person once, and then warn
him a second time. After that, have nothing
to do with him. (Titus 3:10)

There are several kinds of divisive people: 1) Those
who love controversy. They are willing to quarrel on
any subject. 2) Those who deliberately want to divide
believers. They may use slander, gossip, or flattery.
3) Those who seek a following of their own.

# CHAPTER 7

# LOVE

> You shall not bow down to them or worship
> them; for I, the Lord your God, am a jealous
> God, punishing the children for the sin of
> the fathers to the third and fourth generation
> of those who hate me, but showing love to a
> thousand generations of those who love me
> and keep my commandments. (Ex. 20:5-6)

The key word in this passage is not *hate* or *love*. It is *me*.
The important thing is not *that* we love, but *whom* we
love. It is also about how much we love Him: "Jesus re-
plied: 'Love the Lord your God with all your heart and
with all your soul and with all your mind'" (Matt. 22:37).

What does this have to do with unity? Much! Our love
for God is proved by the love we have for our brothers.

> A new command I give you: Love one an-
> other. As I have loved you, so you must love
> one another. By this all men will know that
> you are my disciples, if you love one another.
> (John 13:34-35)

> Above all, love each other deeply, because love
> covers over a multitude of sins. (1 Pet. 4:8)

> We know that we have passed from death to
> life, because we love our brothers. Anyone
> who does not love remains in death. Anyone
> who hates his brother is a murderer, and you
> know that no murderer has eternal life in
> him. (1 John 3:14-15)

## CHAPTER 8

# HUMILITY

Therefore if you have any encouragement
from being united with Christ, if any comfort from his love, if any common sharing in
the Spirit, if any tenderness and compassion,
then make my joy complete by being like-
minded, having the same love, *being one in
spirit and of one mind.* (Phil. 2:1-2)

How can we be of one mind? Paul tells us: through
love, the Spirit, affection, and sympathy. The ESV reads
verse 2 this way: "Complete my joy by being of the same
mind, having the same love, being in full accord and
of one mind." The phrase "full accord" involves two
things: the accord is unanimous, and the unanimity is

not half-hearted. Each person is exuberantly, spontane-
ously in agreement. How is this possible? "Do nothing
from selfishness or conceit, but *in humility count others
better than yourselves.* Let each of you look not only to his
own interests but also to the interests of others. Have
this mind among yourselves which you have in Christ
Jesus" (Phil. 2:4-5 rsv).

*Do nothing from selfishness or conceit.* If we did nothing from selfishness or conceit, we would probably
still be in flat prairie land with nothing plowed. Most
of the motivation in this world comes from selfishness
or conceit. The greatness of the United States today is
based largely on these things, although we give it better names—we call it free enterprise and capitalism.
We commend people who want to be Eagle Scouts,
star football players, Miss Americas, etc., and who
desire those things largely from these two motives.
Very few people want to play in the Super Bowl because whatever they do, they do it unto the Lord. Of
course, there are some who are truly humble and still
get to the top, people that God has put in places of
importance; but they have a major fight on their hands
to keep this from being a problem: Do nothing from
selfishness or conceit.

*But in humility count others better than yourselves.* How
do I do that? What if they are not better than me? Why
should I say they are? Should I lie? No. That would be
false humility.

Years ago, I was responsible for organizing a U.S.
Navy banquet. I had lined up a trumpet player, but he

needed accompaniment, and the pianist didn't show up. One of the guests at the banquet was a very accomplished pianist, so I asked her if she would accompany the trumpeter. Oh no, she couldn't do that, she said. She wasn't good enough. I had known her since she was a little girl, and all she ever did was play the piano. She was very good. But she said she couldn't do it, so I found an eager midshipman who said he could play. He couldn't even play chopsticks. The whole thing was a fiasco. The pianist I had asked first was greatly embarrassed for the man who was playing, and she knew she should have played herself.

When the Bible says, "in humility count others better than yourselves," it does not mean thinking someone is a better pianist when he isn't. Humility does not involve self-deception. True humility means treating others better than you treat yourself. You do not say someone is smarter than you on a certain subject when he is not. What you do is be his servant. *Let each of you look not only to his own interests but also to the interests of others.*

> Let this mind be in you which was also in Christ Jesus, who, being in the form of God, did not consider it robbery to be equal with God, but *made Himself of no reputation*, taking the form of a bondservant, and coming in the likeness of men. And being found in appearance as a man, He humbled Himself and became obedient to the point of death, even the death of the cross. Therefore God

> also has highly exalted Him and given Him
> the name which is above every name, that at
> the name of Jesus every knee should bow, of
> those in heaven, and of those on earth, and of
> those under the earth, and that every tongue
> should confess that Jesus Christ is Lord, to
> the glory of God the Father. (Phil. 2:5-11 NKJV)

When Jesus humbled Himself, He left equality with God to become a man, a servant, and, in effect, a murderer, because He died a murderer's death. He was crucified with two criminals, and many of the people in the first century would not have known the difference between them and Him. Jesus made himself of no reputation. That is the way to unity.

It is also the way to be exalted. In Isaiah 14, when Satan says, "I will be like the Most High; I will exalt myself above the stars; I will be like God," the Bible replies, "But you are brought down to the realm of the dead, to the depths of the pit" (Isa. 14:15). Jesus said, "I will not be like God; I will make myself of no reputation." "Therefore God also has highly exalted him and given Him the name which is above every name" (Phil. 2:9 NKJV). We are to have this mind in us. Selfishness and conceit is the devil's path. Humility is God's. The greatest sin in the Bible is the one which felled the devil and our father Adam—pride. The greatest virtue is the opposite of this sin—humility. The first is the way to division and dissention; the second, to unity. It is very hard to get into fights with humble people.

There are five common types of pride:

- *Pride of face.* Being pleased with your appearance, even though you mostly do not have anything to do with it.

- *Pride of place.* I came from Omaha, and Omaha is obviously the best town in the country—but I didn't have anything to do with that, either.

- *Pride of race.* If you're Dutch, if you're Irish, if you're a blend of six races, whatever you happen to be, you come to the conclusion that that race is the best. But you had nothing to do with that.

- *Pride of grace.* We are glad we're Christians, and we tend to be inordinately pleased with that. We say, "Those pagans next door . . . ," forgetting that God saved us by His grace alone, not for any merits of our own. If it were not for Him, that pagan next door would be *us.*

- *Pride in achievements.* It is easy to take pride in what you have accomplished; but God gave you the body and the brains to do it.

We are all guilty of some of these kinds of pride. One way to recognize them is to periodically take a look at yourself. Romans 12 says that each man should think of himself with sober judgment, no more highly than he ought to think. Sober judgment means looking at yourself the way God does.

God puts people in leadership positions. But when He puts a man into a position of money or power, and that man begins to say to himself, "Oh boy, I am running this show now," or, "I am getting $200,000 a year," that is wrong. Do not be introspective, but keep a sharp eye on how pleased you get with yourself about things like this.

I remember once talking to a chief salesman at an automobile dealership. He was extremely good-looking, with wavy hair graying at the temples and everything in his appearance just right. He was also a gracious Christian; but he knew full well that if he had been ugly, he could not have held that job, even though his appearance had nothing to do with his abilities. His bosses knew he could sell more cars just because of the way he looked. You should take things like this into account and accept them because it is the way God made you, but at the same time do *not* be inordinately pleased with them. Why? Because when we are super-pleased at something like this, we are also displeased with those who are different.

The things that make for true unity are the Lord, the truth of the gospel, love, and humility. The last two are one, because genuine love is not proud.

## CHAPTER 9

# KNOWLEDGE

> Now about food sacrificed to idols: We know
> that we all possess knowledge. Knowledge
> puffs up, but love builds up. (1 Cor. 8:1)

Knowledge leads to pride. Because of this, it can be a cause for disunity. Yet Scripture associates knowledge with truth and wisdom. When the word *knowledge* appears in the Bible, it is almost always the knowledge of God, the Son of God, truth, His will, etc. Is *this* knowledge a cause of disunity? Yes. This is the kind of knowledge that puffs up.

"So then, about eating food sacrificed to idols: We *know* that an idol is nothing at all in the world and that there is no God but one. For even if there are so-called gods, whether in heaven or on earth (as indeed there are many 'gods' and many 'lords'), yet for us there is but one God, the Father, from whom all things came and for whom we live; and there is but one Lord, Jesus Christ, through whom all things came and through whom we live" (1 Cor. 8:4-6). That knowledge is good. However, we can sin against Christ by how we hold on to it. "So this weak brother, for whom Christ died, is destroyed by your knowledge. When you sin against your brothers in this way and wound their weak conscience, you sin against Christ" (1 Cor. 8:11-12).

We teach true knowledge and affirm it as very precious. But do we affirm it *in love* for the brothers? People who hold onto knowledge in a superior way become less like the Lord Jesus.

> If I have the gift of prophecy and can fathom all mysteries and all knowledge, and if I have a faith that can move mountains, but have not love, I am nothing. (1 Cor. 13:2)

> If your brother is distressed because of what you eat, you are no longer acting in love. Do not by your eating destroy your brother for whom Christ died. Do not allow what you consider good to be spoken of as evil. For the kingdom of God is not a matter of eating and drinking, but of righteousness, peace and joy in the Holy Spirit. (Rom. 14:15-17)

Love is senior to knowledge. Knowledge will pass away: "Where there is knowledge, it will pass away" (1

Cor. 13:8b). Love does not pass away: "And now these three remain: faith, hope and love. But the greatest of these is love" (1 Cor. 13:13).

From a very young age, we spend many hours a day in classes, either getting more knowledge or learning how to get it. We are graded on our knowledge. We are promoted because of it. It is a cause for pride. It is difficult not to let it be our highest priority. We do not spend as much time learning about and giving love.

Here are three prayers which combine knowledge and love:

> For this reason I kneel before the Father, from whom his whole family in heaven and on earth derives its name. I pray that out of his glorious riches he may strengthen you with power through his Spirit in your inner being, so that Christ may dwell in your hearts through faith. And I pray that you, being rooted and established in love, may have power, together with all the saints, to grasp how wide and long and high and deep is the love of Christ, and to know this love that surpasses knowledge—that you may be filled to the measure of all the fullness of God. (Eph. 3:14-19)

> And this is my prayer: that your love may abound more and more in knowledge and depth of insight, so that you may be able to discern what is best and may be pure and blameless until the day of Christ, filled with

the fruit of righteousness that comes through
Jesus Christ—to the glory and praise of God.
(Phil. 1:9-11)

For this reason, since the day we heard about
you, we have not stopped praying for you and
asking God to fill you with the knowledge of
his will through all spiritual wisdom and un-
derstanding. And we pray this in order that
you may live a life worthy of the Lord and
may please him in every way: bearing fruit in
every good work, growing in the knowledge
of God, being strengthened with all power
according to his glorious might so that you
may have great endurance and patience, and
joyfully giving thanks to the Father, who has
qualified you to share in the inheritance of
the saints in the kingdom of light. For he has
rescued us from the dominion of darkness
and brought us into the kingdom of the Son
he loves, in whom we have redemption, the
forgiveness of sins. (Col. 1:9-14)

There are divergent views of knowledge within the
body of Christ. Each group thinks that it has revela-
tional truth, "sound doctrine." It is possible that one of
these "knowledges" is truth. It is not possible that all
of them are.

Most people who affirm these distinctive doctrines
are not eager to maintain the unity of the body of Christ.
Each group has schools, colleges, and seminaries for
teaching the rightness of their particular knowledge.

They are eager to maintain the differences. They may not know how to maintain the unity of the Spirit in the bond of peace, but they certainly know how to maintain *disunity*.

Either their knowledge is false, or how they hold to their knowledge is sin, or both. Whichever the case, something needs to be confessed before unity can even be considered.

## CHAPTER 10

# ONE MIND

Finally, brethren, farewell. Become complete.
Be of good comfort, be of one mind, live in
peace; and the God of love and peace will be
with you. (2 Cor. 13:11 NKJV)

All the believers were one in heart and mind.
No one claimed that any of his possessions
was his own, but they shared everything they
had. (Acts 4:32)

The first text is an appeal in the name of the Lord Jesus
Christ. An appeal is a very strong request, just short of
a command. God wants us to agree with one another so
that there will be no divisions among us and so that we
may be perfectly united in mind and thought.

The second text is an example of being of one heart and one mind. The brand-new Christians in Acts were like this. Unity is not something we grow into as we mature in the faith—it is something we start out with that *causes* us to grow to maturity.

The Church's hundreds of years of practice with "maturity" have resulted in more divisions, not fewer. These divisions are sin. "I appeal to you, brothers, in the name of our Lord Jesus Christ, that all of you agree with one another so that there may be *no divisions among you* and that you may be perfectly united in mind and thought" (1 Cor. 1:10). Paul makes this an appeal in the name of the Lord Jesus. He is calling on the highest authority, and he makes it very clear what he is requesting.

We can take one of several approaches to texts like this:

- Let's be real! This is not possible!
- Paul is overstating the requirements.
- "All" doesn't mean "all."
- Let's make it a process.
- There need to be divisions among us to show which of us is right.

"In the following directives I have no praise for you, for your meetings do more harm than good. In the first place, I hear that when you come together as a church, there are divisions among you, and to some extent I believe it. No doubt there have to be differences among you to show which of you have God's approval" (1 Cor. 11:17-19). We need to repent.

## CHAPTER 11

# DISUNITY & CHURCH LEADERS

## Pastors

Keep watch over yourselves and all the flock of which the Holy Spirit has made you overseers. Be shepherds of the church of God, which he bought with his own blood. I know that after I leave, savage wolves will come in among you and will not spare the flock. Even from your own number men will arise and distort the truth in order to draw away disciples after them. (Acts 20:28-30)

Here is a trustworthy saying: If anyone sets his heart on being an overseer, he desires a noble task. (1 Tim. 3:1)

Desiring to be an overseer (a pastor or an elder) is a good thing. Good pastors contribute to unity. However, bad pastors contribute to disunity. If you want to be a pastor or an elder, you must meet the qualifications:

> Now the overseer must be above reproach, the husband of but one wife, temperate, self-controlled, respectable, hospitable, able to teach, not given to drunkenness, not violent but gentle, not quarrelsome, not a lover of money. He must manage his own family well and see that his children obey him with proper respect. (If anyone does not know how to manage his own family, how can he take care of God's church?) He must not be a recent convert, or he may become conceited and fall under the same judgment as the devil. He must also have a good reputation with outsiders, so that he will not fall into disgrace and into the devil's trap. (1 Tim. 3:2-7)

> To the elders among you, I appeal as a fellow elder, a witness of Christ's sufferings and one who also will share in the glory to be revealed: Be shepherds of God's flock that is under your care, serving as overseers—not because you must, but because you are willing as God wants you to be; not greedy for money, but eager to serve; not lording it over those entrusted to you, but being examples to the flock. And when the Chief Shepherd appears, you will receive the crown of glory that

will never fade away. Young men, in the same
way be submissive to those who are older.
All of you, clothe yourselves with humility
toward one another, because, "God opposes
the proud but gives grace to the humble." (1
Pet. 5:1-5)

## Teachers

"It was he who gave some to be apostles, some to be
prophets, some to be evangelists, and some to be pastors and teachers, to prepare God's people for works of
service, so that the body of Christ may be built up until
we all reach unity in the faith and in the knowledge of
the Son of God and become mature, attaining to the
whole measure of the fullness of Christ" (Eph. 4:11-13).
Between the words *teachers* and *unity* are the people
who are prepared to build up the body. Many teachers
teach the truth but only prepare their flocks to listen to
and follow them. They do not prepare Christians for
works of service. The result is that the body is not built
up into the unity of the faith.

There are also teachers like the ones in Ephesus who
distort the truth to get people to follow them: "Even from
your own number men will arise and distort the truth
in order to draw away disciples after them" (Acts 20:30).

Others teach biblical truth, commands, and promises, but they do not teach *obedience* to the commands
or *trust* in the promises. It is easier to teach informa-
tion than it is to teach belief and obedience. Many

teach theologies that do not agree with other theologies. These teachers are eager to retain disunity in the body. They think this kind of teaching is a virtue. Other teachers simply do not practice what they preach.

The followers imitate the teachers.


## Pastors-Teachers-Evangelists

You probably know (or are at least familiar with) what pastors, teachers, and evangelists are supposed to do. Here is one responsibility that may surprise you. Paul said God gave these people "to prepare God's people for works of service, so that the body of Christ may be built up until we all reach unity in the faith and in the knowledge of the Son of God and become mature, attaining to the whole measure of the fullness of Christ" (Eph. 4:12-13).

Pastors, teachers, and evangelists are the prime movers in bringing people to unity, knowledge, maturity, and fullness. God's people are the secondary movers as they lead others into this. Pretty neat, huh? The problem is that pastors, teachers, and evangelists are trying to do all the works of service themselves instead of preparing God's people to do them.

## CHAPTER 12

# FALSE UNITY

Not all unity is good, and not all divisions are bad. Some people desire unity so much that they think it is primary. It is not. There are right reasons for division, and there are wrong reasons for unity. Unity is very, very important, but it is not so important that you are to maintain it at the expense of the truth of the gospel.

> I marvel that you are turning away so soon from Him who called you in the grace of Christ, to a different gospel, which is not another; but there are some who trouble you and want to pervert the gospel of Christ. *But even if we, or an angel from heaven, preach any other gospel to you than what we have preached*

*to you, let him be accursed.* As we have said before, so now I say again, if anyone preaches
any other gospel to you than what you have
received, let him be accursed. (Gal. 1:6-9 NKJV)

When we see something supernatural, we tend to
believe it. But Paul says supernaturality has nothing
to do with truth. "We or an angel from heaven." If the
angel Gabriel came through the ceiling right now in
all his glory and told you that salvation was by doing
good works or by standing on your head in a corner,
he would be in trouble. If the Apostle Paul himself
preached a different gospel to us than the one that
we received and that brought us to the Savior, then *he*
would be in trouble. "Let him be accursed." Paul did
not care who was preaching it. Incidentally, this is the
only place in the Scripture where a double curse is pro-
nounced. "As we have said before, *so now I say again,* if
anyone preaches to you a gospel contrary to that which
you received, *let him be accursed*" (Gal. 1:9).

"Am I now seeking the favor of men or of God, or
am I trying to please men? If I were still pleasing men,
I should not be a servant of Christ" (Gal. 1:10). False
unity says we've got to please. It says that pleasing *men*
will bring us unity. But if I spend my time trying to
please men, I am not being a servant of Christ.

"You were running well; who hindered you from
obeying the truth? This persuasion is not from him
who calls you. A little leaven leavens the whole lump. I
have confidence in the Lord that you will take no other view than mine; and he who is troubling you will

bear his judgment, whoever he is. But if I, brethren, still preach circumcision, why am I still persecuted? In that case the stumbling block of the cross has been removed" (Gal. 5:7-11 RSV). The cross is a dividing line. Paul calls it a stumbling block. Christian unity must be in the cross, so if the cross causes divisions, so be it. If pleasing men at the expense of obeying God brings unity, *not* so be it. True Christian unity is grounded in the gospel alone.

You cannot have real unity if you compromise truth. However, there is a ditch on the other side, too. You can hold onto the truth in the wrong way. If you say that your theology is of first importance down to all the details, you end up not loving Christians who differ with you on those details. The truth can also be a stumbling block if our eagerness to communicate it makes us forget to love the people we are communicating it to. (Likewise, trying to be loving can make us neglect speaking the truth.)

Where do you draw the line between the gospel and the details of Christianity? If you think of truth as a body of doctrinal statements, you are missing the point. Instead, think of the truth as embodied in the person of the Lord Jesus Christ: "Jesus said to him, 'I am the way, and the truth, and the life'" (John 14:6a RSV).

When we think of truth as the creed of a certain church, we put our trust in doctrine rather than in Jesus Christ. When we speak the truth, it should be an expression of our relationship with the Lord. The truth is an act (the gospel) and a person (Jesus), and our words are just its expression. The Truth was the Son of God who came to lay down His life for us. The act was an act of love, His death on the cross. Jesus did not come down to earth and say, "Okay, here it is, one, two, three . . . " He came and *did* something, and that something was love.

Unity is based on the truth of the gospel, in love. It should be impossible for us to give the message of the cross without getting wrapped up in Jesus. Sadly, many people can spout the gospel as a dry-as-dust, unloving, merely doctrinal explanation of what Christ did. When you tell the gospel as bare "truth," not as love, the Good News becomes bad news. It is like putting the gospel through a sieve: you keep the words and leave the Lord behind.

Another kind of union that is not the unity of the Spirit is the unity of co-belligerents. These are people who have a common enemy—e.g. Russia and the U.S. at war with Germany or Roman Catholicism, Mormonism, and evangelical Christianity standing against abortion and gay marriage.

Peace-loving at the expense of purity is false unity. This was the case with Neville Chamberlain's agreement with Nazi Germany before World War II. It was "peace in our time," i.e. peace at any cost. What God calls us to have is *righteousness* at any cost. The cost was the Son of God. His death broke down the wall between Jews and Gentiles. It breaks down all other barriers, too. "Therefore, since we have been justified through faith, we have peace with God through our Lord Jesus

Christ, through whom we have gained access by faith into this grace in which we now stand" (Romans 5:1).

Before I close the chapter, I would like to discuss one last kind of union that can present itself as unity— ecumenism. The ecumenical movement is the attempt to establish worldwide Christian unity by drawing the Protestant and Eastern Orthodox churches closer together. It centers primarily in the World Council of Churches. It was preceded by several evangelical movements in the nineteenth century: The World's Young Men's Christian Association, founded in 1878, The World's Young Women's Christian Association in 1894, the World's Student Christian Association in 1895, and the Student Volunteer Movement.

The modern word "ecumenism" came from the World Missionary Conference in 1910 in Edinburgh, Scotland. At that conference, the movement was hijacked by the liberal theology of the Student Christian Movement. Here is a quotation from John Stott's book *The Cross of Christ*:

> The first was the disaffiliation in 1910 of the Cambridge Inter-Collegiate Christian Union (founded in 1877) from the Student Christian Movement (founded in 1895). CICCU[5] members were conscious of standing in the tradition of Bilney, Tyndale, Latimer, Ridley and Cranmer, the great names of the Cambridge Reformation. They also looked back with pride and affection to Charles Simeon, who

5  Cambridge Inter-Collegiate Christian Union

for fifty-four years (1782-1836) as vicar of Holy Trinity Church had faithfully expounded the Scriptures and, as his memorial plaque testifies, "whether as the ground of his own hopes or as the subject of all his ministrations, determined to know nothing but Jesus Christ and him crucified." It is not surprising, therefore, that they were becoming increasingly disenchanted with the liberal tendencies of the SCM, and especially with its weak doctrines of the Bible, the cross and even the deity of Jesus. So when Tissington Tatlow, general secretary of the SCM, met the CICCU members in March 1910, the vote to disaffiliate the Union was taken. The following year Howard Mowll (later to be archbishop of Sydney and primate of Australia) became president of CICCU and helped to establish it on firm evangelical foundations from which it has never been moved.

After the First World War ended in 1918, many ex-servicemen went up to Cambridge as students. CICCU by now was much smaller than the SCM. Yet the SCM leaders (notably Charles Raven, the dean of Emmanuel) made overtures to the CICCU, hoping that they would rejoin and supply the missing devotional warmth and evangelistic thrust. To resolve the issue, Daniel Dick and Norman Grubb (president and secretary of CICCU) met the SCM committee in the rooms in Trinity Great Court of the secretary, Rollo Pelly.

Here is Norman Grubb's own account of the crucial issue:

After an hour's talk, I asked Rollo point-blank, "Does the SCM put the atoning blood of Jesus Christ central?" He hesitated, and then said, "Well, we acknowledge it, but not necessarily central." Dan Dick and I then said that this settled the matter for us in the CICCU. We could never join something that did not maintain the atoning blood of Jesus Christ as its centre; and we parted company.[6]

Jonathan Goforth also mentions the 1910 World Missionary Conference in his book, *By My Spirit*:

Was there ever such an incomparable opportunity for Christian leaders to get rid of their ecclesiastical idols and bring themselves into heart contact with the unsearchable riches of Christ as at the Missionary Conference in Edinburgh in 1910? There has been no Church gathering in modern times around which such expectations have centered. Missionary leaders had come from all parts of the world. It was the confident hope of many that a new era in missions has dawned. The subject for the last day was—"The Home Base." It provoked visions of endless possibilities. The home churches, empowered by a mighty Holy Ghost Revival, would send out men

6  Stott, John R.W. *The Cross of Christ*. Downers Grove, Illinois: IVP Books, 2006, p. 14.

fitted as were Paul and Barnabas. With their enormous resources in men and means the world would be evangelized in a generation.

Alas! it was only a dream. Never have I experienced such keen pain and disappointment as I did that day. Of the many who addressed that great missionary gathering, not more than three emphasized God the Holy Spirit as the one essential factor in world evangelization. Listening to the addresses that day, one could not but conclude that the giving of the Gospel to lost mankind was largely a matter of better organization, better equipment, more men and women. Symptoms, indeed, were not lacking that a few more sparks might have precipitated an explosion. But no, the dethronement of the idol of ecclesiastical self-sufficiency was apparently too great a price to pay.[7]

The ecumenical movement is a false unity.

Biblical, godly, Christ-exalting oneness already exists in the body of Christ. We are one body. This is not ecumenism. Ecumenism speaks of false union, and this is not at all what we are talking about. There is no compromising of the basic truth that our Lord Jesus prayed about—no "playing footsie" under the table with those who are

7  Goforth, Jonathan. *By My Spirit*. Nappanee, Indiana: Evangel Publishing House, 1983, pp. 137-8.

traitors to the message of the cross, the blood of Christ and the resurrection of our Lord. That would be intolerable.[8]

8 Palau, Luis. "Working Together." Lecture delivered at Urbana '79.

## CHAPTER 13

# TRADITION

> You have let go of the commands of God
> and are holding on to the traditions of men.
> (Mark 7:8)

Every church has rituals and traditions. Certain traditions are easy to recognize (Amish, Mennonites, and Quakers, for example). These traditions are not just quaint culture. They are deadly to the gospel, even if some members of the tradition are truly saved. A white-cap Mennonite can be kicked out of the church simply for having fellowship with a black-cap Mennonite, and vice versa. The Amish will not have fellowship with the Quakers, or the Quakers with the Baptists. They have made their traditions of first importance. In doing so, they are denying the gospel: "There is neither Jew nor Greek, slave nor free, male nor female, for you are all one in Christ Jesus" (Gal. 3:28). We cannot have complete unity until these traditions are confessed and forsaken.

Many Christian churches whose traditions are less recognizable than the ones mentioned above still consider them more important than the gospel. Here are a few examples.

In 1948, I became closely acquainted with a Disciples of Christ chaplain in the Navy. He held very strongly to baptism by immersion and taking the Lord's Supper every Lord's Day. He held to them not because he thought they were *biblical*, but because *that is what his church always did*. As I remember, he did not believe in the inspiration of Scripture, the virgin birth, or the resurrection of Jesus.

In 1973, I was on a panel for Washington State University where a Lutheran theologian was the speaker. He was an ordained Lutheran pastor who served communion. In his talk, he said that the only things we definitely knew about Jesus were that he was baptized by a man named John and that he had fellowship with people who were down and out. It did not bother me that he did not believe in Jesus. What bothered me was that despite the fact that he did not believe in the deity of Christ, *communion* was very important to him. It was his tradition.

Most traditions are extra-biblical, but they are still considered authoritative, although they differ from church to church. There is no way we can have unity without recognizing that the way we hold to these extra-biblical traditions is sin and confessing and forsaking them. This is not likely to happen without the conviction of the Holy Spirit.

What about biblical traditions? God instituted the Passover to be done annually as a remembrance of the exodus from Egypt. It was replaced with the Lord's Supper. Traditions such as these are good, if you are actually doing them to remember. It matters *why* you do, not just *what* you do. Tradition for the sake of tradition is sin, even when the tradition is based on biblical truth.

> "The multitude of your sacrifices—what are they to me?" says the Lord. "I have more than enough of burnt offerings, of rams and the fat of fattened animals; I have no pleasure in the blood of bulls and lambs and goats. When you come to appear before me, who has asked this of you, this trampling of my courts? Stop bringing meaningless offerings! Your incense is detestable to me. New Moons, Sabbaths and convocations—I cannot bear your evil assemblies. Your New Moon festivals and your appointed feasts my soul hates. They have become a burden to me; I am weary of bearing them. When you spread out your hands in prayer, I will hide my eyes from you; even if you offer many prayers I will not listen. Your hands are full of blood." (Isa. 1:11-15)

The sacrifices Isaiah spoke of were biblical. Who started these traditions? God started them. But the people forsook Him in their hearts and in their manner of living while still holding onto the traditions.

At worst, rituals become idolatrous; at best, figures of the true. Between the best and the worst, they are dead traditions. Normally they start as figures of true things and end up as idols. The rituals described in detail in the Old Testament were meant to be figures of the true (see Hebrews 7-10). Long before these rituals were fulfilled in Jesus Christ, they had ceased to be figures; they became the real thing to the people who practiced them. When this happened, they were no longer acceptable to God.

There is an example of this when Jesus used the bronze serpent to open up the gospel to Nicodemus in John 3:14. "Just as Moses lifted up the snake in the desert, so the Son of Man must be lifted up." This bronze serpent, the symbol of sin and death, also symbolized Jesus who was made sin for us. This true figure of the cross became an idol to the people for seven hundred years until Hezekiah had it destroyed. "He removed the high places, smashed the sacred stones and cut down the Asherah poles. He broke into pieces the bronze snake Moses had made, for up to that time the Israelites had been burning incense to it. (It was called Nehushtan.)" (2 Kings 18:4).

Do not do anything just because it was done before. When I was a student at the Naval Postgraduate School in Monterey, California, my wife and I were members of the First Baptist Church in downtown Monterey. Occasionally the pastor would ask me to preach. A group of the men in the church decided to construct a building in a suburb of Monterey called Seaside. They wanted to started a Sunday school there with the intention of making it a full church later on. While they were working on the building, they asked me to hold a prayer meeting with the workers every Wednesday night.

When the building was completed, they thought, "Why just have a Sunday school? Why don't we start the Sunday school and the church at the same time?" Since I was conducting their prayer meeting, they asked if I would pastor the church as long as I was still a student at the graduate school.

I said, "We'll have to have an order of service."

They said, "We'll have the same order of service that the main church has."

I said, "No."

"What's wrong with it?"

"Nothing's wrong with it, but you don't do anything just because that's the way it was done before. Give it another 300 years, and you'll have the same problems as the Catholic Church."

I am acquainted with many different church traditions, but I am very familiar with two conservative, evangelical denominations—Southern Baptist and Missouri Synod Lutheran. Although they are very different from each other, both are gospel-preaching churches. Consequently, there are saved people in both. However, the traditions of each denomination keep many of their own people from getting saved. I am not going to make a case for that here. Please check it out.

What are your "traditions"? Have they lost their significance?

## CHAPTER 14

# READER COMMENTS

**#1**

Jim, you are probably going to deal with this, but I think the greatest incentive for unity is Christ's "High Priestly Prayer" in John 17; especially verses 22-23.

"I have given them the glory that you gave me, that they may be one as we are one: I in them and you in me. May they be brought to complete unity to let the world know that you sent me and have loved them even as you have loved me" (John 17:22-23).

The unity of the Body is one of the most forceful apologetics for the divinity of Christ.

Conversely, disunity is Satan's most success-
ful tool.

I think I mentioned on our visit that the
Greek word from which we get "heresy" has
the root meaning of division.

In Him,
Otto Helweg

Amen! Because of Otto drawing my attention to John
17, I entitled this book *I Have Given Them the Glory.* Otto
went into the presence of the Lord in 2008.


**#2**

Is it possible, and if so how, to tell if someone
else is not a part of the body, as opposed to
someone "acting like" they are not a part of
the body?

If someone who calls himself a Christian is not acting like it, you can assume he is not a Christian because:

- He does not show love to the brothers (1 John 3:14).

- He does not obey God's commands (1 John 2:3).

- He has the works of the flesh and not the fruit of
  the Spirit (Gal. 5:19-24).

- He may not understand spiritual truth (1 Cor. 2:14).

However, a man may call himself a Christian and
even remember when he was converted, and you may
remember years when he had evidence of salvation. I

start by assuming such a person *is* a Christian even if present evidence is lacking. Christian friends and elders should seek to get him to repent and confess every sin that he committed since his conversion. If he comes back into joy, peace, and obedience, then he was a Christian all the time.

If he confesses his sins and still has no joy, or if he does not confess, we should treat him as an unbeliever who needs Christ. However, since he *says* he is a Christian and is not repentant, we have an obligation to bring church discipline on him: "But now I am writing you that you must not associate with anyone who *calls himself a brother* but is sexually immoral or greedy, an idolater or a slanderer, a drunkard or a swindler. With such a man do not even eat" (1 Cor. 5:11).

For more on this subject, please see Appendix A on assurances of salvation.

#3

> Personally, I have never understood how any
> professing Christian can be a racist. I am sure
> you have known some as well as I have. The
> passages referenced in this devotional make it
> obvious. If the twelve Apostles had been racists,
> then no Gentile would have ever been saved!

I have known a few, and we can find them in the New Testament as well. Peter was a racist at the beginning of Acts 10 and in Galatians 2: "When Peter came to Antioch, I opposed him to his face, because he was clearly in the wrong. Before certain men came from James, he used to eat with the Gentiles. But when they arrived, he began to draw back from the Gentiles because he was afraid of those who belonged to the circumcision group. The other Jews joined him in his hypocrisy, so that by their hypocrisy even Barnabas was led astray" (Gal. 2:11-13).

Paul wrote to racists in Rome and Ephesus in his letters. These were international churches with attendant racial problems. Paul gave teachings and commands to correct them. We find it easier to avoid the problems and the requirement for teaching obedience by being in separate churches. That way we can hang on to our prejudices while convincing ourselves that we do not have any.

# CONCLUSION

Before we can apply what we have learned from the Bible about unity, we need to know the basic truths of Scripture. Believing these truths does not make them true. They are true anyway. Here are a few about Christians:

> Therefore, if anyone is in Christ, he is a new creation; the old has gone, the new has come! (2 Cor. 5:17)

> But now that you have been set free from sin and have become slaves to God, the benefit you reap leads to holiness, and the result is eternal life. (Rom. 6:22)

> I have been crucified with Christ and I no longer live, but Christ lives in me. The life I live in the body, I live by faith in the Son of God, who loved me and gave himself for me. (Gal. 2:20)

> And you also were included in Christ when you heard the word of truth, the gospel of your salvation. Having believed, you were marked in him with a seal, the promised Holy Spirit. (Eph. 1:13)

> But the fruit of the Spirit is love, joy, peace, patience, kindness, goodness, faithfulness, gentleness and self-control. Against such things there is no law. Those who belong to Christ Jesus have crucified the sinful nature with its passions and desires. (Gal. 5:22-24)

These Scriptures are true for all born-again Christians. If they do not describe you, the reason is very simple: you are not saved. Even if you are a church member, it will be impossible for you to apply the teaching on unity because you are not part of the body of Christ.

I have included an appendix on assurances of salvation drawn from the New Testament. If the assurances describe you, it is both possible and imperative that you apply the Scriptures on unity. As an individual member of the body of Christ, you cannot act as if you were the whole congregation. However, you need to obey God even if your church does not.

1. Admit that you are not obeying. Confess this disobedience as sin.

2. Confess all other sins you have not confessed since you were saved.

3. Choose to obey. Ask God for an opportunity to obey and the grace to do it.

# ASSURANCES OF SALVATION

There is a minimum of truth without which a person cannot be saved. This is the gospel.

> Now, brothers, I want to remind you of the gospel I preached to you, which you received and on which you have taken your stand. By this gospel you are saved, if you hold firmly to the word I preached to you. Otherwise, you have believed in vain. For what I received I passed on to you as of first importance: that Christ died for our sins according to the Scriptures, that he was buried, that he was raised on the third day according to the

Scriptures, and that he appeared to Peter, and
then to the Twelve. (1 Cor. 15:1-5)

Here is the basic truth of the gospel:

- Who Jesus is—He is the Christ.
- Christ died for our sins according to the Scripture.
- He was buried. His burial did two things: It
  confirmed His death (He was dead *and buried*.),
  and it confirmed His resurrection.
- He was raised on the third day according to the
  Scripture.

This is the truth that saves. Believing any less than
this will not result in salvation.

*1: It is possible to know that you are saved.*
"I write these things to you who believe in the name
of the Son of God so that you may know that you have
eternal life" (1 John 5:13). 1 John was written so that you
may know that you have eternal life. Do you want to
know? Read the letter twice. Then go through it a third
time and mark every occurrence of the word "know."
It will show up with two different meanings, but mark
them all. Each verse will tell you how you can know
that you have eternal life.

*2: The Holy Spirit is a means of knowing.*

> We know that we live in him and he in us, be-
> cause he has given us of his Spirit. (1 John 4:13)

> The Spirit himself testifies with our spirit that
> we are God's children. Now if we are chil-
> dren, then we are heirs—heirs of God and co-
> heirs with Christ, if indeed we share in his
> sufferings in order that we may also share in
> his glory. (Rom. 8:16-17)

God's Spirit talks to our spirit to tell us that we belong to Him. We are His children. I cannot explain it,
but to those to whom this has happened it does not
need explaining.

The Holy Spirit is the present guarantee of our final
salvation, the resurrection of our bodies:

> And you also were included in Christ when
> you heard the word of truth, the gospel of
> your salvation. Having believed, you were
> marked in him with *a seal, the promised Holy
> Spirit*, who is a deposit guaranteeing our in-
> heritance until the redemption of those who
> are God's possession—to the praise of his
> glory. (Eph. 1:13-14)

> Now it is God who has made us for this very
> purpose and has given us the *Spirit as a de-
> posit, guaranteeing what is to come*. (2 Cor. 5:5)

We either have the Spirit or we do not have the Spirit. Whoever does not have the Spirit does not belong to
Christ. He is not a Christian. He is not saved.

> You, however, are controlled not by the sinful
> nature but by the Spirit, if the Spirit of God

lives in you. *And if anyone does not have the Spirit of Christ, he does not belong to Christ.* (Rom. 8:9)

. . . those who are led by the Spirit of God are sons of God. (Rom. 8:14)

Have you been led by the Spirit? That is supernatural guidance. If you have not been led by the Spirit or if you have and do not recognize it, you should wonder if you are saved.

For who among men knows the thoughts of a man except the man's spirit within him? In the same way no one knows the thoughts of God except the Spirit of God. We have not received the spirit of the world but the Spirit who is from God, that we may understand what God has freely given us. This is what we speak, not in words taught us by human wisdom but in words taught by the Spirit, expressing spiritual truths in spiritual words. *The man without the Spirit does not accept the things that come from the Spirit of God, for they are foolishness to him, and he cannot understand them, because they are spiritually discerned.* The spiritual man makes judgments about all things, but he himself is not subject to any man's judgment: "For who has known the mind of the Lord that he may instruct him?" But we have the mind of Christ. (1 Cor. 2:11-16)

The natural man may be a genius, but unless he has the Spirit of God, the Word of God is foolishness to him.

## 3: Change of character

"The acts of the sinful nature are obvious: sexual immorality, impurity and debauchery; idolatry and witchcraft; hatred, discord, jealousy, fits of rage, selfish ambition, dissentions, factions and envy; drunkenness, orgies, and the like. I warn you, as I did before, that those who live like this will not inherit the kingdom of God" (Gal. 5:19-21). If this list describes your normal state, you will not inherit the kingdom of God.

"But the fruit of the Spirit is love, joy, peace, patience, kindness, goodness, faithfulness, gentleness and self-control. Against such things there is no law. Those who belong to Christ Jesus have crucified the sinful nature with its passions and desires. Since we live by the Spirit, let us keep in step with the Spirit" (Gal. 5:22-25). If this describes you, you are saved. Jesus saves out of the first list into the second list. If you find yourself in both lists at the same time, it is for one of the following reasons.

You are mistaking natural personality traits for the fruit of the Spirit. It is not. The fruit of the Spirit is the characteristics of God given to a person when he is saved.[9]

You are saved but are deliberately choosing to go back into the first list. Confess and forsake it right now.

9  How do you tell the difference? Well, what happens when a trial comes? A person who is naturally friendly can easily be mistaken for someone who is filled with the fruit of the Spirit of love. But what happens when he comes across someone who is very hard to love? Is he able to love him? The fruit of love does not depend on the loveliness of the person being loved, whereas the person who only has the personality trait will run out of love. (Of course, many Christians *act* like non-Christians by not loving the unlovely. The difference is that they *could* love the unlovely if they chose to, but the natural man could not.)

You are naturally in the first list but faking the second list. That is, you are a hypocrite. You are not saved.

*4: Confessing Jesus as Lord*

> Therefore I tell you that no one who is speaking by the Spirit of God says, "Jesus be cursed," and no one can say, "Jesus is Lord," except by the Holy Spirit. (1 Cor. 12:3)

> That if you confess with your mouth, "Jesus is Lord," and believe in your heart that God raised him from the dead, you will be saved. For it is with your heart that you believe and are justified, and it is with your mouth that you confess and are saved. (Rom. 10:9-10)

This confession is not a matter of the mouth only. People who do not have the evidence of the Holy Spirit say it in liturgies all of the time. It must come from the heart. "A good man brings good things out of the good stored up in his heart, and an evil man brings evil things out of the evil stored up in his heart. For the mouth speaks what the heart is full of" (Luke 6:45).

*5: Obedience*

> No one who lives in him keeps on sinning. No one who continues to sin has either seen him or known him. (1 John 3:6)

> No one who is born of God will continue to sin, because God's seed remains in him; he

cannot go on sinning, because he has been born of God. This is how we know who the children of God are and who the children of the devil are: Anyone who does not do what is right is not a child of God; nor is anyone who does not love his brother. (1 John 3:9-10)

We know that anyone born of God does not continue to sin; the one who was born of God keeps him safe, and the evil one cannot harm him. (1 John 5:18)

We know we are saved because we are no longer living in sin. If it looks like we are living in sin, then there is no reason for others to know that we are Christians, and no reason for us to, either. "We know that we have come to know him if we obey his commands" (1 John 2:3). Obedience is not the means of salvation; it is evidence of our salvation. Are you obedient?

## 6: Discipline

If obedience is a means of knowing that you know the Lord, what happens when you disobey?

And you have forgotten that word of encouragement that addresses you as sons: "My son, do not make light of the Lord's discipline, and do not lose heart when he rebukes you, because the Lord disciplines those he loves, and he punishes everyone he accepts as a son." Endure hardship as discipline; God is treating you as sons. For what son is not disciplined by his father? *If you are not disciplined* (and everyone undergoes discipline), *then you are illegitimate children* and not true sons. Moreover, we have all had human fathers who disciplined us and we respected them for it. How much more should we submit to the Father of our spirits and live! Our fathers disciplined us for a little while as they thought best; but God disciplines us for our good, that we may share in his holiness. No discipline seems pleasant at the time, but painful. Later on, however, it produces a harvest of righteousness and peace for those who have been trained by it. (Heb. 12:5-11)

God does not discipline those who are not His children. If you are getting away with disobedience, you are not a child of God. If you are being disciplined, pay attention and repent. It is evidence that you are saved.

## 7: Loving Christians

"We know that we have passed from death to life, because we love our brothers. Anyone who does not love remains in death" (1 John 3:14). Christians love non-Christians. Non-Christians love non-Christians. It takes a Christian to love a Christian.

In her autobiography, *Climbing*, Rosalind Goforth tells of an elderly man who was unsure of his salvation. He said, "I wanted to convince myself all these years that I'm going to heaven, but I can't."

She asked him if he loved the Lord's people.

He said, "Oh, it's my greatest joy in life to be with the Lord's people on the Lord's day singing the Lord's praises."

She pointed him to 1 John 3:14: "We know that we have passed from death to life, because we love our brothers." Love for the brothers is evidence of salvation.

Consider the opposite. Suppose you brought a non-Christian to church. He would not feel comfortable. He might admire and respect Christians, but he won't love them like they love each other. He cannot. Jesus said that the pagans love pagans and that Christians are to love pagans; but it takes a *Christian* to love a Christian.

When you love other Christians, not only do you know that you are saved—everyone else also knows: "A new command I give you: Love one another. As I have loved you, so you must love one another. By this all men will know that you are my disciples, if you love one another" (John 13:34-35).

## 8: Loving Enemies

> But to you who are listening I say: Love your enemies, do good to those who hate you, bless those who curse you, pray for those who mistreat you. If someone slaps you on one cheek, turn to them the other also. If someone takes your coat, do not withhold your shirt from them. Give to everyone who asks you, and if anyone takes what belongs to you, do not demand it back. Do to others as you would have them do to you. If you love those who love you, what credit is that to you? Even

sinners love those who love them. And if
you do good to those who are good to you,
what credit is that to you? Even sinners do
that. And if you lend to those from whom you
expect repayment, what credit is that to you?
Even sinners lend to sinners, expecting to be
repaid in full. But love your enemies, do good
to them, and lend to them without expecting
to get anything back. Then your reward will
be great, and you will be children of the Most
High, because he is kind to the ungrateful
and wicked. Be merciful, just as your father
is merciful. (Luke 6:27-36)

## 9: Jesus said so

"I tell you the truth; whoever hears my word and believes him who sent me has eternal life and will not
be condemned; he has crossed over from death to life"
(John 5:24). Notice the present tense: hears my word, believes in Him who sent me, has eternal life. Notice the
future tense: will not be condemned. Notice the past
tense: he *has* crossed over from death to life.

# THE TRUE CHURCH

*by J.C. Ryle*

I want you to belong to the one true Church: to the Church outside of which there is no salvation. I do not ask where you go on a Sunday; I only ask, "Do you belong to the one true Church?"

Where is this one true Church? What is this one true Church like? What are the marks by which this one true Church may be known? You may well ask such questions. Give me your attention, and I will provide you with some answers.

The one true Church is composed of all believers in the Lord Jesus. It is made up of all God's elect—of all converted men and women—of all true Christians. In whomsoever we can discern the election of God the Father, the sprinkling of the blood of God the Son, the sanctifying work of God the Spirit, in that person we see a member of Christ's true Church.

It is a Church of which all the members have the same marks. They are all born again of the Spirit; they all possess "repentance towards God, faith towards our Lord Jesus Christ," and holiness of life and conversation. They all hate sin, and they all love Christ. They worship differently, and after various fashions; some worship with a form of prayer, and some with none; some worship kneeling, and some standing; but they all worship with one heart. They are all led by one Spirit; they all build upon one foundation; they all draw their religion from one single book—that is the Bible. They are all joined to one great centre—that is Jesus Christ. They all even now can say with one heart, "Hallelujah;" and they can all respond with one heart and voice, Amen and Amen.

It is a Church which is dependent upon no ministers upon earth, however much it values those who preach the gospel to its members. The life of its members does not hang upon Church membership, or baptism, or the Lord's Supper—although they highly value these things, when they are to be had. But it has only one Great Head—one Shepherd, one chief Bishop—and that is Jesus Christ. He alone, by His Spirit, admits the members of this Church, though ministers may show the door. Till He opens the door no man on earth can open it—neither bishops, nor presbyters, nor convocations, nor synods. Once let a man repent and believe the gospel, and that moment he becomes a member of this Church. Like the penitent thief, he may have no opportunity of being baptized; but he has that which is far better than any water-baptism—the baptism of the Spirit. He may not be able to receive the bread and wine in the Lord's Supper; but he eats Christ's blood by faith every day he lives, and no minister on earth can prevent him. He may be excommunicated by ordained men, and cut off from the outward ordinances of the professing Church; but all the ordained men in the world cannot shut him out of the true Church.

It is a Church whose existence does not depend on forms, ceremonies, cathedrals, churches, chapels, pulpits, fonts, vestments, organs, endowments, money, kings, governments, magistrates or any act of favor whatsoever from the hand of man. It has often lived on and continued when all these things have been taken from it. It has often been driven into the wilderness, or into dens and caves of the earth, by those who ought to have been its friends. Its existence depends on nothing but the presence of Christ and His Spirit; and they being ever with it, the Church cannot die.

This is the Church to which the scriptural titles of present honor and privilege, and the promises of future glory especially belong; this is the Body of Christ; this is the flock of Christ; this is the household of faith and the family of God; this is God's building, God's foundation, and the temple of the Holy Ghost. This is the Church of the firstborn, whose names are written in heaven; this is the royal priesthood, the chosen generation, the peculiar people, the purchased possession, the habitation of God, the light of the world, the salt and the wheat of the earth; this is the "Holy Catholic Church" of the Apostles' Creed; this is the "One Catholic and Apostolic Church" of the Nicene Creed; this is that Church to which the Lord Jesus promises "the gates of hell shall not prevail against it," and to which He says, "I am with you alway, even unto the end of the world" (Matt. 16:18, 28:20).

This is the only Church which possesses true unity. Its members are entirely agreed on all the weightier matters of religion, for they are all taught by one Spirit. About God, and Christ, and the Spirit, and sin, and their own hearts, and faith, and repentance, and necessity of holiness, and the value of the Bible, and the importance of prayer, and the resurrection, and judgment to come—about all these points they are of one mind. Take three or four of them, strangers to one another, from the remotest corners of the earth; examine them separately on these points: you will find them all of one judgment.

This is the only Church which possesses true sanctity. Its members are all holy. They are not merely holy by profession, holy in name, and holy in the judgment of charity; they are all holy in act, and deed, and reality, and life, and truth. They are all more or less conformed to the image of Jesus Christ. No unholy man belongs to this Church.

This is the only Church which is truly catholic. It is not the Church of any one nation or people; its members

are to be found in every part of the world where the
gospel is received and believed. It is not confined within the limits of any one country, or pent up within the
pale of any particular forms or outward government. In
it there is no difference between Jew and Greek, black
man and white, Episcopalian and Presbyterian—but
faith in Christ is all. Its members will be gathered from
north, and south, and east, and west, and will be of
every name and tongue—but all one in Jesus Christ.

This is the only Church which is truly apostolic. It is
built on the foundation laid by the Apostles, and holds
the doctrines which they preached. The two grand ob-
jects at which its members aim are apostolic faith and
apostolic practice; and they consider the man who talks
of following the Apostles without possessing these two
things to be no better than sounding brass and a tin-
kling cymbal.

This is the only Church which is certain to endure
unto the end. Nothing can altogether overthrow and
destroy it. Its members may be persecuted, oppressed,
imprisoned, beaten, beheaded, burned; but the true
Church is never altogether extinguished; it rises again
from its afflictions; it lives on through fire and water.
When crushed in one land, it springs up in another. The
Pharaohs, the Herods, the Neros, the bloody Marys,
have labored in vain to put down this Church; they slay
their thousands, and then pass away and go to their
own place. The true Church outlives them all, and sees
them buried each in his turn. It is an anvil that has broken many a hammer in this world, and will break many

a hammer still; it is a bush which is often burning, and yet is not consumed.

This is the only Church of which no one member can perish. Once enrolled in the lists of this Church, sinners are safe for eternity; they are never cast away. The election of God the Father, the continual intercession of God the Son, the daily renewing and sanctifying power of God the Holy Ghost, surround and fence them in like a garden enclosed. Not one bone of Christ's mystical Body shall ever be broken; not one lamb of Christ's flock shall ever be plucked out of His hand.

This is the Church which does the work of Christ upon earth. Its members are a little flock, and few in number, compared with the children of the world: one or two here, and two or three there—a few in this parish and a few in that. But these are they who shake the universe; these are they who change the fortunes of kingdoms by their prayers; these are they who are the active workers for spreading knowledge of pure religion and undefiled; these are the life-blood of a country, the shield, the defense, the stay, and the support of any nation to which they belong.

This is the Church which shall be truly glorious at the end. When all earthly glory is passed away then shall this Church be presented without spot before God the Father's throne. Thrones, principalities, and powers upon earth shall come to nothing; dignities, and offices, and endowments shall all pass away; but the Church of the first-born shall shine as the stars at the last, and be presented with joy before the Father's throne, in the day of Christ's appearing. When the Lord's jewels are made up, and the manifestation of the sons of God takes place, Episcopacy, and Presbyterianism, and Congregationalism will not be mentioned; one Church only will be named, and that is the Church of the elect.

Reader, this is the true Church to which a man must belong, if he would be saved. Till you belong to this, you are nothing better than a lost soul. You may have the form, the husk, the skin and the shell of religion, but you have not got the substance and the life. Yes, you may have countless outward privileges; you may enjoy great light and knowledge—but if you do not belong to the Body of Christ, your light and knowledge and privileges will not save your soul. Alas, for the ignorance that prevails on this point! Men fancy if they join this church or that church, and become communicants, and go through certain forms, that all must be right with their souls. It is an utter delusion; it is a gross mistake. All were not Israel who were called Israel, and all are not members of Christ's Body who profess themselves Christian. Take notice; you may be a staunch Episcopalian, or Presbyterian, or Independent, or Baptist, or Wesleyan, or Plymouth Brother—and yet not belong to the true Church. And if you do not, it will be better at last if you had never been born.

*Ryle preached this sermon in 1858.*